MYSTE
OF THE ANCI

C000176922

THE QUEST
FOR TROY

DONALD EASTON

WEIDENFELD & NICOLSON

LONDON

The stories of Troy and the Trojan War are known throughout the Western world, and have been the subject of innumerable paintings, sculptures and works of literature. The stories go back to a body of legends which circulated in

*A*ttic vase, 490–480 BC, showing the Achaean
warriors Achilles and Agamemnon.

classical times and are set in a heroic age, when Greece

and Anatolia (modern Turkey) were divided into small

kingdoms ruled by warrior-kings.

Paris, son of Priam King of Troy (in Anatolia), had abducted the fabulously beautiful Helen, wife of Menelaus, King of Sparta (in Greece). In revenge, a coalition of Greek ('Achaean') kings set sail with 1,000 ships to raid the cities of Anatolia and besiege Troy. After ten years the siege was finally broken by a Greek ruse. Pretending to depart, they left behind a wooden horse, apparently a thank-offering to the gods; the Trojans took the horse into their city where, after nightfall, Greeks emerged from the horse's belly, opened the gates to the attackers and Troy was sacked and burned. It was a brutal victory which, however, left the Greek participants disoriented and rootless and led to the eventual collapse of the heroic age and its civilization.

Homer's Iliad

Historians in Ancient Greece mainly placed the Trojan War somewhere in the period 1250–1135 BC, and some elements of the story may go back to the 2nd

millennium BC, but crucial in bringing together some of the legends and elaborating them was the Greek poet Homer (*c.*730 BC). Homer did not include the full story of the Trojan War in the *Iliad*. He did not, for example, include the wooden horse,

Warriors depicted on a vase from Mycenae, early 12th century BC.

Bust of Homer, now in the Louvre, 2nd century BC.

phron la ville de Troie

la porte Dardane

although clearly this part of the legend was current at the time, as it is depicted on a vase from Mykonos dated *c.*670 BC. Other parts of the body of legends were drawn on by other writers, most notable among whom is Virgil, the Roman poet who wrote the *Aeneid c.*30–19 BC. to celebrate the supposed descent of the Romans from the Trojans.

At some stage the *Iliad* was committed to writing, after which it must have been copied countless times; the earliest manuscripts to survive intact come from the 10th century AD, from Constantinople. The first printed edition of Homer was produced in Florence in 1488. And so the stories of Troy and the Trojan War passed into European culture, where they became deeply embedded.

But what is the historical reality behind them? Was there a city called Troy? And did the Trojan War ever really happen?

Exploration

Homer's epic poem places Troy on the Asiatic side of the Dardanelles Straits, opposite the Gallipoli peninsula. Here, on a low ridge 5 km from the sea, the inhabitants of the classical city of Ilion (730 BC onwards) believed that they lived on the site of ancient Troy. Although their city was destroyed *c.* AD 500, the name of Troy remained current in the area. Medieval travellers were shown a variety of ruins along the coast and believed that they had seen Troy.

Seventeenth-century travellers were more critical, and noticed that Homer places Troy on an inland plain, which they began to explore. The first positive suggestion for locating the site of Troy came in 1784 from Jean-Baptiste Lechevalier, who had been taking part in a French survey of the north-east

F *rench illustration of the 15th century depicting the Trojan horse. The Trojan War was a frequent theme in medieval romances.*

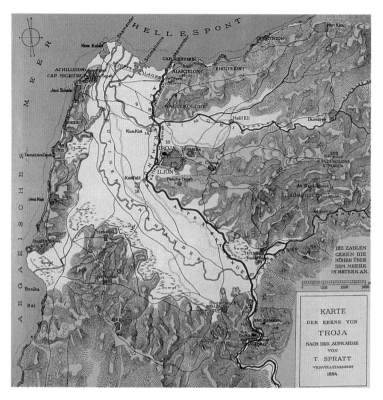

KARTE
DER EBENE VON
TROJA
NACH DER AUFNAHME
VON
T. SPRATT
VERVOLLSTÄNDIGT
1894

DIE ZAHLEN
GEBEN DIE
HÖHEN ÜBER
DEM MEERE
IN METERN AN.

M *ap of the Troad: the northwest tip of Asiatic Turkey.*

V *iew from the classical site at Pınarbaşı, before Schliemann, generally accepted as the location of Homer's Troy.*

Aegean. At the south end of the plain he discovered a hill above a village called Pınarbaşı. The hill had traces of ancient settlement, four burial-mounds and lay between a river and a group of springs feeding a small stream. In the river and stream Lechevalier saw Homer's rivers Simois and Scamander, in the burial-mounds he saw those of the heroes of the *Iliad*, and on the hill he placed Troy. It was a convincing identification which held the field for nearly a century.

In further survey-work in 1793, an engineer called Franz Kauffer noted a site on a ridge much closer to the sea and known to the Turks as Hisarlık. After being shown coins and inscriptions, the Cambridge mineralogist Edward Daniel Clarke correctly identified this in 1801 as classical Ilion. So the generally accepted view became that classical Ilion lay at Hisarlık while the earlier, 'Homeric' Troy lay at Pınarbaşı.

*A*erial view of
Hisarlık from
the South. Originally
an oval-shaped
mound, it now bears
the scars of more
than 25 seasons of
excavation.

*V*iew of Hisarlık from the Trojan Plain.

There were, however, dissenting voices. The earliest of these was the founder and editor of *The Scotsman*, Charles Maclaren. In an essay in the *Edinburgh Review* in 1820 he argued that the stream below Pınarbaşı was too

small to be Homer's Scamander and that if, as Homer implies, Troy lay between two rivers, it could only have been at Hisarlık. This argument placed Troy on the site of classical Ilion – precisely where the ancient inhabitants and most of their contemporaries believed it to have been.

Maclaren's view, re-worked and re-published in 1863, attracted the attention

Heinrich Schliemann in his mid-fifties. Portrait by Sydney Hodges.

The citadel walls and ramp of Troy II, c.2400 BC, as exposed in Schliemann's excavations in 1873.

of a British resident of the Troad, Frank Calvert, who happened to own a part of Hisarlık. In test excavations in 1863 and 1865 he found that Pınarbaşı was a purely classical site, but that Hisarlık had deep deposits of earlier occupation. This convinced him of the likelihood of Maclaren's identification, but he lacked the money to take the matter further. In 1868, however, he succeeded in interesting a wealthy traveller in the site, and persuaded him to start large-scale excavations. That traveller was Heinrich Schliemann (1822–90).

Excavation

The site at Hisarlık was an oval mound approximately 220 m long and 15 m high, resulting from the collapse and rebuilding of successive mudbrick and stone buildings repeated over millennia.

Schliemann dug there briefly in 1870 and then in 1871–3, 1878–9, 1882 and 1890. As a newcomer to archaeology he was largely ignorant of its logic

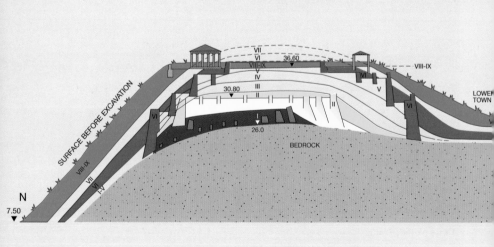

View of Schliemann's north–south trench. Exposed in the bottom are walls of Troy I, c.3000 BC.

and methods, and his early work was lamentably crude. But it improved over the years, and (unusually for his day) he had the wit to engage the help of professional draughtsmen, photographers and scientists – and a brilliant architect.

His excavations removed the core of the mound to a depth of 10 m (in places 15 m) and in the accumulation of strata he distinguished nine broad phases. Schliemann stopped digging at 10 m deep, because here he found impressive mudbrick buildings, all burnt, with rich collections of gold, silver and bronze metalwork. He assumed that this was Priam's Troy, the Troy of the Trojan War.

Schliemann died in 1890, and his architect Wilhelm Dörpfeld continued the excavations in 1893–4. Dörpfeld concentrated on the southern rim of the mound, mainly left intact by Schliemann. Here he found monumental stone buildings of a later date, far more impressive than those found by Schliemann. Some of the pottery, of a type known from Mycenaean sites in Greece, enabled these buildings to be dated to *c.*1400–1200 BC, the putative period of the Trojan War.

Dörpfeld's work gave him a clear picture of the structure of the site. Repeated building had increased the size of the mound upwards and outwards, but the top had been sliced off to build a Roman temple-platform, most of which had subsequently been robbed by local peasants. Thus the remaining ruins appeared as a series of concentric rings, the innermost being the earliest.

Schematic section through the citadel mound of Troy (Dörpfeld, revised by Korfmann).

17

New excavations were sponsored in 1932–8 by the University of Cincinnati, under Carl Blegen. It was a model excavation for its day, and resulted in a model publication in 12 large volumes. Blegen sampled all periods of the site's development by digging in disconnected areas untouched by Schliemann or Dörpfeld. This produced a much refined understanding of the sequence of artefacts and buildings, Blegen observing over 40 phases where Schliemann had seen nine. There was, however, some difficulty in making precise correlations between his findings and those of his predecessors.

Since 1988 there have been new excavations by an international team under Professor Manfred Korfmann of Tübingen University. It is an enormous project with over 100 archaeologists, making extensive use of modern scientific and technological methods. In the mound Korfmann is recovering a continuous

*P*rofessor Manfred Korfmann (centre) discusses the site with other members of the Troy team.

*F*allen architectural piece being moved after having been drawn and photographed.

THE
QUEST
FOR
TROY

*E*xcavation in
*progress, 1992.
One archaeologist
might work with four
to six workmen.*

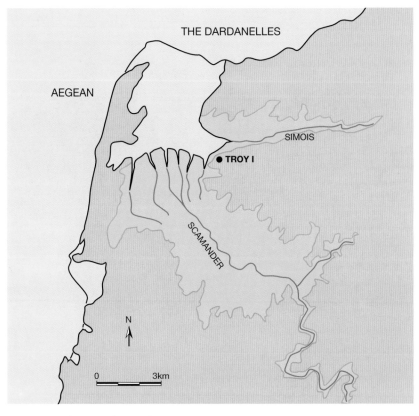

sequence of strata from all periods by enlarging Schliemann's deepest and longest trench. This will provide a useful check on earlier work. He is also digging widely in the area surrounding the mound. Here a lower town of Hellenistic and Roman date has long been known to exist, but the new excavations have shown that under it there is also an entire lower town of prehistoric date. This has revolutionized our view of pre-classical Troy.

3,500 Years of Occupation

When Hisarlık/Troy was founded, before *c*.3000 BC, the ridge on which it stood was surrounded by water. What is now the Trojan Plain was then a bay with its mouth just inside the entrance to the Dardanelles, and it was so

Areas last dug by Schliemann

Areas last dug by Dörpfeld

Areas last dug by Blegen

Areas last dug by Korfmann (up to 1995)

*M*ap showing the existence of a bay in Troad in prehistoric times.

*P*lan to show who last dug where on the citadel mound of Troy.

throughout prehistory. This was Troy's greatest asset; adverse currents and winds made it extremely difficult for ships to negotiate the Dardanelles, and the bay provided a harbour where they could await a favourable wind. Troy was able to profit.

Occupation on the site is still conventionally divided into nine broad phases. Initially (Troy I, c.3000–2600? BC: all dates are still under discussion) the settlement consisted of a small group of adjoining mudbrick long-houses

surrounded by a stone circuit-wall. In Troy II (*c*.2600–2150? BC) it developed into a well-built citadel with 10-metre-

***P**aved stone ramp, c.2400 BC, which led up to the principal gate of the Troy II citadel.*

high fortifications approached by a paved ramp and heavily-defended gates. This was a period of economic growth made possible partly by the introduction of the wheel. Metallurgy blossomed, and from this period come most of the 21 'treasures' found by Schliemann. Within the citadel was a 35-metre-long temple or audience-hall flanked by two parallel buildings, all standing within a colonnaded courtyard with a ceremonial gateway. After a devastating fire *c*.2350 BC, the citadel interior was covered with a maze of houses and streets – a pattern which, despite another fire, continued into Troy III (*c*.2150–2000? BC). A lower town existed but its size is presently unknown.

*S*treet leading through the lower town of Troy VI–VII to a gate in the citadel wall.

The next phases, IV–V (*c*.2000–1700? BC), are not so well known but appear to have been periods of quiet development. But in Troy VI (*c*.1700–1280? BC) the site reached its apogee. There was now a magnificent fortress defended by beautifully built stone walls and towers and filled with monumental stone palaces. A lower town surrounded by ditch and palisade extended 400 m to the South. The pottery suggests that there were close contacts with Mycenaean Greece. The artistic traditions of Troy VI survived destructions *c*.1280 and 1200 BC (VIIa), to continue at a somewhat impoverished level (Troy VIIb, *c*.1200–1000? BC). Signs of influence from Thrace may reflect the arrival in Anatolia of the Phrygians.

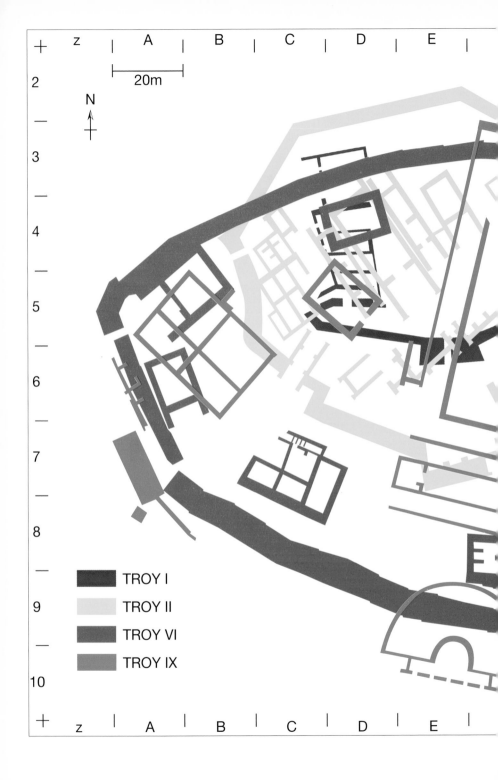

z	A	B	C	D	E		

20m

N

TROY I
TROY II
TROY VI
TROY IX

*S*implified
plan of
the principal
buildings on
the citadel
mound of Troy.

*T*rojan pottery of various periods.

*R*oman concert-hall or odeion, *renovated by the* **Emperor Hadrian. Originally the seating extended much higher.**

A period of abandonment followed, during which the ruins of VI and VII remained visible. These perhaps became the focus of stories about the Trojan War. Then, *c.*730 BC, around the time of Homer, the citadel was rebuilt (Troy VIII) by Greek colonizers. With other cities in the northern Troad, they formed themselves into a league, erected an up-to-date theatre, temple and council chamber at Troy, and sponsored periodic games, which became an attraction to pilgrims and tourists from far and wide.

The city was attacked and burnt in 85 BC; but Rome, which regarded Troy as its mother-city, invested heavily in rebuilding (Troy IX). Most public buildings were renewed, and a water-system was installed. The city was destroyed by earthquakes towards the end of the 5th century AD, and was only sparsely inhabited thereafter.

Trésor de Priam découvert à 8½ mètres de profondeur

Missing Treasure

A mystery has surrounded the most famous finds from the excavations, Schliemann's 'treasures', which disappeared from the Berlin museums in May 1945 and vanished without trace.

These 'treasures' were 21 groups of metalwork: hoards of jewellery, vessels, weapons, tools and other items of gold, silver, bronze and semi-precious stones, mostly from Troy II. The largest was 'Priam's Treasure' – so called because Schliemann thought that it must have been a royal treasure and that the

The Troy II hoard of gold, silver and bronze objects found by Schliemann at Troy in 1873 – conventionally but wrongly known as 'Priam's Treasure'.

Gold vessels from 'Priam's Treasure.' The purpose of the 'sauceboat' is unknown: it may have been a loving-cup or a libation-vessel.

stratum from which it came was that of the Trojan War. It has been suggested that the discovery was a hoax, and that the treasure was compiled by Schliemann from scattered finds or purchases; but the evidence is weak and the theory has little to commend it. It was almost certainly a genuine hoard, but we now know that it came from earlier than Schliemann thought: it was deliberately buried *c.*2150 BC, nearly 1,000 years before the date usually given to the Trojan War.

Schliemann's excavation permit required him to share his finds with the Imperial Museum in Constantinople, but he smuggled most of them out of Turkey to his house in Athens. The Turks brought a case against him in the Greek courts (1874–5), which Schliemann effectively won by hiding his collection. Turkey reluctantly accepted financial compensation and apparently relinquished all claim to the objects.

Schliemann first exhibited his Trojan antiquities, including the treasures, at the South Kensington (now the Victoria and Albert) Museum in London from 1877 to 1880. He then gave them as an outright gift to the German nation, and they were exhibited in Berlin from 1882. He continued to add to them as new discoveries were made and by a massive bequest at his death in 1890.

At the outbreak of war in 1939, the Berlin museums put the most valuable items from the Troy treasures into three specially made boxes. After initial storage in museum and bank strong-rooms, in November 1941 the boxes were taken to a supposedly bomb-proof anti-aircraft tower at the Berlin Zoo. This tower was surrendered to the Red Army on 1 May 1945. The Director of the Museum of Pre- and Early History, who after the war was eventually given a senior archaeological post in East Berlin, is said to have claimed

Replica of gold earring from 'Priam's Treasure.' Similar earrings were exported from Troy to other cities in the north-east Aegean.

Ceremonial axes from Troy II. One is made from lapis lazuli which must have come from Afghanistan.

in private that he had personally handed the boxes over to a high-level Soviet commission; but few knew of this, and its truth was in any case doubted.

A chance documentary discovery in Moscow in 1987 revealed that at the end of the war the Soviet Union had pursued a policy of taking 'restitution in kind' for German looting and destruction of Soviet art works in 1941–4. A Red Army 'Trophy Brigade' of art historians had indeed taken the boxes from the anti-aircraft tower in May 1945, and had sent them by plane to Moscow. In Moscow they were held in complete secrecy by the Pushkin State Museum of

Fine Arts until 1994, when a small number of western scholars (including the author) were invited to examine them.

The objects went on public display in April 1996, and remain in the Pushkin Museum. Their future is uncertain as there are impending claims for ownership from Turkey and Germany.

Has Troy Been Found?

Schliemann thought that the burnt citadel and treasures of Troy II were proof of the Trojan War's historicity. Dörpfeld thought the same of Troy VI, and Blegen of Troy VIIa. But since these three phases have little in common but their destruction, their arguments come back to a belief in the correctness of the location.

Despite all the exploration and excavation, it has never been proved that Hisarlık is the site of Homer's Troy. The only conclusive proof would be a pre-classical inscription naming the site or giving some other unmistakable indication, and such an inscription has not yet been found. But Hisarlık is in the right general location, it was an important city in pre-classical times, and its later occupants believed they were living on the site of ancient Troy. This all makes it a very good candidate.

There may be contemporary evidence for the existence of Troy from the archives of the Hittite Empire (*c*.1600–1200 BC) at Boğazköy in Central Turkey. Among the names of places in Western Anatolia known to the Hittites is a pair which occur together: Tarwisa and Wilusa. These may be the Anatolian names underlying the Greek pair Troy and Ilios (or Ilion). Hittite texts also mention an Aegean power known to them as Ahhiya (or Ahhiyawa), perhaps the Achaean Greeks; but it is not clear where Tarwisa and Wilusa lay, and the Trojan War itself is not referred to.

*T**he Hittite
capital
Hattusa, modern
Boğazköy, in
central Turkey.*

Temple area of the lower town of the Hittite capital Hattusa, modern Boğazköy.

Although excavation has produced no texts to prove the historicity of the Trojan War, is the archaeology nonetheless consistent with it? For this, Troy would need to have a burnt layer of the right date. If the Trojan War took place in the 13th century BC, and the Achaean Greeks were what we now call Mycenaeans, then Troy VI (destroyed *c.*1280 BC) would be a very good candidate. Blegen attributed its destruction to an earthquake, but on very thin evidence. Another possible candidate is Troy VIIa (destroyed *c.*1200 BC); but this phase seems to have outlived a general disintegration of Mycenaean power, so its destruction by a massive coalition of Mycenaean Greeks is not easily conceivable.

The site of Hisarlık suffered many destructions throughout its history, and

The inner face of the Troy VI citadel wall (right) leans over to the north. Blegen saw this as evidence for an earthquake in Troy VI.

an earlier historical origin to the legend is also possible. Linguistically some verses in the *Iliad* predate the Mycenaean Linear B texts of the 13th century; and already in the 15th century the Hittites may have known an Anatolian song about Wilusa, possibly the same place as Troy. The Trojan War could have taken place in the 15th century or before.

We are dealing with three different classes of evidence: from literature, history and archaeology. The three are not easy to relate. The Trojan War is known only from literature. History and archaeology neither confirm nor deny its historicity. They allow us to believe in it if we wish; but it still remains unproved.

THE
QUEST
FOR
TROY

PHOTOGRAPHIC ACKNOWLEDGEMENTS
Cover AKG London; pp. 2–3, 4, 5, Peter Clayton
[PC]; p. 6 AKG; pp. 8, 8–9 Donald Easton [DE];
pp. 10–11 Troia Project/Professor Manfred
Korfmann [TP]; pp. 12–13 DE; pp. 14, 14–15
AKG; pp. 16t, 18 © Hartmut Schickert;
pp. 19, 20–21 DE; p. 24 PC; pp. 25, 28t, 28–29 TP;
p. 30 PC; pp. 31, 33 AKG; p. 24 Novosti Photo
Library; pp. 36–7, 38 E.T. archive; p. 39 DE.

First published in Great Britain 1997
by George Weidenfeld and Nicolson Ltd
The Orion Publishing Group
5 Upper St Martin's Lane
London WC2H 9EA

Text copyright © Donald Easton, 1997
The moral right of the author has been asserted
Design and layout copyright © George Weidenfeld
and Nicolson Ltd, 1997

A CIP catalogue record for this book is available
from the British Library
ISBN 0 297 822713

Picture Research: Suzanne Williams

Designed by Harry Green

Typeset in Baskerville